I0187266

The National Poetry Review
Issue Number Eleven

Editor:
C. J. Sage

Assistant Editors:
Ashley Capps
Jill Alexander Essbaum

Contributing Editor:
T. R. Hummer

Subscriptions:

Individuals: $15 per year
Institutions: $25 per year
(Please add $6 for subscriptions outside the United States)

Address **subscriptions** to:

Subscriptions
The National Poetry Review
Post Office Box 2080
Aptos, California 95001-2080

**TNPR reads magazine submissions in email only.
Please see website for the latest guidelines and reading periods.**

For prize offerings and detailed submission guidelines, please visit
www.nationalpoetryreview.com

The National Poetry Review is distributed in the United States and Canada by Ingram Periodicals,
and indexed by *Humanities International Complete* and *The Index to American Periodical Verse*.

The National Poetry Review Copyright 2003, 2004, 2005, 2006, 2007, 2008, 2009. 2010, 2011, 2012
All rights reserved
ISBN 978-1-935716-11-2
ISSN 1543-3455

Cover Art:

That Pink Line by Mary Zeran
acrylic on cradled panel
www.maryzeran.com

Poetry

Book Reviews: 27

Essay: 35

Editorial Outside Ourselves: 44

About the Contributors: 49

United States Whip Company Complex

But we, and the very tops of our hills

Oh, and if only for chance moments

But she shot me directly in the twig

And I'm a big dummy for believing it

But in those days even the music boxes.

Our cataclysm, our accessories

On a mission narrowly averted

Two precious self-portraits

Swabbing at our duhs, these

Excruciating thingies

But she kicked me in my speaking part

Squarely in the script

Should we be sitting still for portraits

Else moment-to-moment shrugs

Autumn is such degradation

And I Europe and you do, too

Like we were nothing, birds are kind of not

Friendly, look they fly away.

Vanishing Point

I might be obsessed

with smallness. Sometimes

I want to yell "Macaroni!"

but then I feel void of meaning.

How about you give me meaning

and vice versa. How about

you're the doctor and I'm your

subject. I want your subject

to like my subject. I like

your mouth but I can't hear

a word you're saying. I'm just saying,

if existence were an endless line,

a heart monitor, you might be my biggest

blip. I might be a crater. I might be

wrong. Last wrong turn

I ended up in Dubuque

on the world's shortest trolley.

At the top of the hill, I could still

see my green flip-flops melting

into the asphalt. They were small,

very small. Perspective

is a big deal. It's as big

as a baby's arm. It's bigger than

the bones they found buried

beneath the old drive-in theatre.

I remember making out there

in the back seat, your hands,

my green soccer shorts. I remember

the shorts! It's always the little things.

A man carves a Marilyn Monroe

so small that she fits in the eye

of a needle. No needle will prevent you

from shrinking entirely. It appears

you are becoming smaller

from here, in The Future.

I think you had blue eyes.

I can't see your face from this distance.

You appear to be merging with

the tree down the street.

Live Light

There are lines at the station,

everyone wonders what's holding

things up. A big question

pops out of the frost cabbages,

getting slowly and methodically

vague. The lines continue

to grow. Everyone is waiting

for something. Why won't it come?

Some of us gesticulate to ourselves.

A passerby embraces another passerby;

he knew her somehow, he said,

from a distant life. I was spending

all my time trying to decipher

the backgrounds of things

and this was driving me back.

A stone wheel in the ground

wouldn't rotate in any direction

so we remained without direction,

waiting. Is it true that each instant

happens for a reason, and must

this be believed? I am sitting here

drinking too much for a reason.

She's walking across the street

for no apparent reason

for a reason. It seems temporary,

this spot on the earth which stands

for eons. When my son was born,

I was smoking in the hospital lot.

Five meteorites shot out of themselves

and I watched them. Time at times

can strike like a loose bandoleer

in the dead of night; then was unusually bright,

the tails of meteors like strings of glass

illuminating things small animals share.

Is this the best I can do? One easily

forgets; what kind of light

does it take. History, at times, at least

for an instant, glances back.

Spelling Bee

I mumble to myself more and more
saying things aloud to no one
even when folks are around.
Don't know if it is because my hair
is falling out or because I have
a disease. There are flowers
inside the mind and they don't
have to be geraniums or lilacs
or skunkweed they can just
be flowers. It's National
Ice Sculpture time of the year,
I just learned, while fumbling
along a treadmill at the gym
where sometimes in the locker room
I say something inadvertent
to the locker, that a trabant
is a kind of squire, or something.
Also, xerarch means 'can grow out
of dryland', which I know because
I know a word called xerophyte.
It's kind of unfair—what spelling
wiz kid doesn't know all the X words.
There are only a handful of them,
but the Ts, heck. The cute little guy

who missed trabant and had to return

through the black tunnel

probably would have nailed xerarch.

Then again no, maybe not;

a lot of the X words sound like Zs,

like when I was a kid. They had

to drill it into the small pasta meat

of my head that xylophone starts with x, not z.

I should know that; I've played it

my whole life. I'm talking about the spirit

of competition. It's about what you draw

and how you use what you draw,

and if you start talking to yourself

you might as well learn

some obscure and lovely words

and offbeat professions like

sculptor, train photographer, drag-boat

racer, onion scientist. Collider operator.

Julie Danho

Abstraction

On the screen, blacks and whites

expand contract/expand contract,

like mouths trying to force words out.

In this murk, she looks for a body,

comes up empty. I know the possibilities:

it's too early or it never was.

I could hang these images on a wall,

name them, "Moon," "Clouds,"

"Volcano Taken From Above."

The answers always have our faces.

For years I didn't want to be a mother—

now need swells like a tick.

I wait to see if it takes shape,

or if what I'm left is this:

a sheet of white, quiet on the line

The Part of Summer That's Easy to Talk About

They were hemlocks,

I think. The boy and his father

sawed away the sick

branches. That's what I saw

but I can't even say

what kind of trees

they were, so

you shouldn't listen

to me. I don't listen

to me either. On one branch,

a crow staggered

and lazily flicked its wings

to keep balance

until the father had

severed the last inch.

Then it flew to another

tree. You can't saw

down that crow, I thought,

and the boy caught

the branch below

and chewed it up

with his machine.

Go Back, Pilgrim

Remembering is a steep climb
to a box sealed in granite.
Raise your eyes. There is new weather
heading east. Hand over hand
is best. Call out my name and I may
hear you. A volcano lived there.
You can slip on basalt. I know
your shoulders ache.
Take a seat next to the past.
Here are all the nouns: people,
places, and things. Verbs
are actions, but frozen. Here
are the 50s, before interstates.
The family is driving to Nebraska.
You may join them if you wish.
On the way to Kindergarten, your
mother holds your hand. Curtie
died of polio, but there he is.
A girl named Alice. Look
for your birth in the corner.
Here comes language, waking up
on the savannah. New oceans
pour on boiling rock.

Mythology

The albino deer comes every day now,

suckles on the bird feeder like a baby

nursing as we stand behind the window

inventing its life, which, we all agree,

is not a good life, must be a lonely

life, because the other deer with their smooth

brown flanks move in a ballet only

they know, and our strange thing does not move

with them, and even the dog knows it's not the same,

doesn't bark, as if to say there is nothing worse

than loneliness and what kind of game

would it be to chase what has already been cursed,

and now we're closing the shutters, and now

we're turning away from the window.

Winner of the Finch Prize for Poetry

Edison Dupree

Shaker

You're right, the world is lost. But wait—
here on the table this pepper alone
until you shake it
is night and stars by the million,

your dream vacation in space—
all your body's sad comedy suddenly weightless,
tumbling along, the way lost satellites do.
Nowhere they have to be…

And afterward, whatever the hand has earthquaked
up, that little grey storm
out there beyond the crook of the arm,
is yours. You wrecked it.

Strike

Imagination saying No
said nothing, so
I struck a match,

and watched the fire mutely
eat backward
from the match head,

till head and blackened
neck bowed down,
trying to pray with ash for brains,

me for god
and these for words.

Heather Kirn

Deserted Base

The township stripped
     the border of barbed wire,
now calls this grass a park.
     This land made bombs and blue-
prints for a cold war
     we only fought as little balls
that hid beneath the desks.
     Still nice to be walking,
the two of us agree,
     on open space. I don't say
failure or premature
     ovarian, egg-less or ran out
before she started
     trying. The sky is winter-
stone, the ground, green
     frost. She and I are in the zone
we never thought we'd trespass.
     These acres once told us,
top secret, toxic, plot
     your three-mile way around.
The navy and its base got
     between us. Pennies in our shoes
pinched us home, and we twirled
     phone chords to the ever

after of eighteen-years-old.

      Now we see our mothers'
linoleum split-levels

      and the short space between
them: new knowledge on old

      terrain. Like traversing past
the scent of another on a lover's

      wrist. Like learning a birth-
mark of a body in the casket.

      Like hearing that your heart
of thirty years beats a little

      broken. Like, like
—when we were girls—rolling

      back the chestnut drawer
to find in the middle of her

      home was hidden the quiet,
pregnant angle of a gun.

      We don't say *remember*
when, don't risk recalling

      her blood's susurrus (faint
as naval waves that interfered

      with radios) that never said to stop
naming futures—*Amber*,

      Benjamin—while we chalked
horses on asphalt and jets

      flew overhead. But she says,
I can still carry,

and I hear the verb lack

its predicate, the arms

of the Rs hold their own

withholding, vacant

as this field that once was home

to planes, idle, waiting.

Poem Recording a Lawn Party in Winter

The raccoon had no business dying in Joe's swimming pool.

The balance is all fucked up. It's spring in January, a spiking

74 degrees and blooming. The kind of weather calling for brunch

and laundry lines, so Tony layers lox and red onion on a salt bagel

in his backyard while his blue-striped boxers finger the breeze that fingers us.

Whitney uproots a 16-inch radish from the middle of the lawn,

and it's so long and carrot-like Tony assures us they'll use it later in bed,

and Whitney responds by buttering, cubing and serving it up

in a porcelain bowl. *There's evidence, she says, that in the end science*

will meet Nature head on at the far side of something like a field.

Everything wants to make a connection, and Nature's hard, but given

the chance Whitney prefers to be eaten alive by dinosaurs.

Frank and Cherie's son claws his way around croquet brackets catching lizards.

His little sister confesses he sometimes kills them and Joe

suggests making lizard soup, laughs aloud at himself and I'm surprised

by how obvious it is that he's childless; Tony hands out

post-brunch dental floss and we begin flossing in our lawn chairs

while the kids bring picked blossom after blossom to Cherie,

who looks lovely in flora. But the flossing makes us pensive, and Tony recalls

a dead armadillo in his driveway that resembled a dinosaur

which he found repulsive and which he refused to touch or bury,

making Whitney double-bag it. He then ran, I mean ran blocks

to dump it in the park trash can where it stunk up a hell of a radius waiting

for the sanitation man. It makes sense Tony will have no part helping

Joe dispose of the drowned raccoon. *You're such a pussy*, Joe tells him,

and Tony immediately cops to it. *Look at it as Karmic opportunity*,

Frank says, and his son nearly clocks him with a croquet ball on accident

while his daughter impales her stuffed bunny on one of the rainbow

shafted stakes. Later, at home, Joe smokes a hunk of turkey pastrami,

wearing thick rubber gloves. He handles it as he would a woman, sliding his fingers over its curves, licking the spice rub, nibbling a piece here

and there, and I think, if it weren't for killing and eating, he'd kiss it.

Behind the house, in private, I shovel a square of earth, slicing through

marbled roots and centipedes. Fishing the raccoon from the pool

with a foil baking pan, I'm struck by the weight of it in my pink arms.

A thin smell of rot diffuses through my painter's mask but only one

hind paw shows decay and its eyes are so cataracted they're baby blue.

When it rains at night Tony calls and says he hopes that raccoon

doesn't unearth itself and come washing back into our lives like the undead,

which is to say, the living.

Picturesque Rendering That Attempts to Chill

Everything suddenly started "mellowing" at the same time,
and no, that's not the sound a cat makes. It's what happens

when all wherewithal has dissolved. The motel rooms
don't even bother having doors, and the ice machine churns

solid bricks the size of a bathtub, because who really
needs pieces? Isn't that just selfish? A camera falls apart

into a sink, and tourists try to wash it down rather than face
humiliation. I went to the junior prom in a homespun

dress of aluminum foil and film stripped from canisters,
which are not those little shakers that make me want to deck

the gypsy lady on the bus, but a plastic sarcophagus born
just for film, back in the days of film. They got rid of film

because it was so dangerous. A negative could flutter down
from the rafters at the most inopportune time, such as

during surgery, or a difficult intimate maneuver. The bumper
sticker told everyone to mellow, but nobody cared to obey.

A Coin-Operated Button-Down Collar

You had a job in accounting. You had a wide skein
of pink broadcloth, claimed it as an inheritance, but
who on earth would tax it, as every bee on earth died
for sins committed without the slightest flower. Your
mother held up the convenience store on my street.
She used you as the getaway driver. Nobody shoveled
that neighborhood out. Too bad you hadn't been born.
Of course she really didn't steal anything. There was
no section for sewing notions. Our mothers wanted
nothing but the entire royal wedding. The drinks they
invented while they neglected us. I worked myself all
the way through the storm sewer, only missed when
I wasn't there to fetch more grenadine. You used
the word math like it was a sexual innuendo. Some
tailor closed down shop with exactly zero dollars.

Mary Oliver, *Swan*. Bloodaxe, 2010, 96pp, $22
Reviewed by Douglas Basford

When, in one of her notebook entries, Mary Oliver declares Thoreau to be "overly social," it is not hard to hear her siding squarely with Emerson, who, after the famous transparent-eyeball line in "Nature," articulates how if one truly enters into a state of nature, even the sound of the name of an intimate friend is estranging: "to be brothers, to be acquaintances, master or servant is then a trifle and a disturbance." So severe is her solitude that, as she says in one of her poems in *Swan*, her most recent collection, "If you have ever gone into the woods with me, I must love you very much." Ironically, of course, she has taken all of us, many thousands of us, her greatest fans and her most pointed detractors alike, into the woods and onto sea shores on what Frost would have termed her news-finding missions. Some of the most startling moments in her poems, though, come from when she breaks her self-imposed isolation to wonder about the lives of others, such as in "This Day, and Probably Tomorrow Also" in *Red Bird* (2008), where she goes from an interjection about versifying experience ("What an elite life!") to a vision of happenstance around the world:

> While somewhere someone is kissing a face that is crying
>
> While somewhere women are walking out, at two in the morning—
>
> many miles to find water
>
> While somewhere a bomb is getting ready to explode.

Unfortunately for Oliver, this move proves only *locally* startling, as others from Auden to Rich, from Heaney to Clifton having more terrifyingly, winningly forced us to confront the instabilities of the ethics and usefulness of our making in the face of overwhelming political realities. The earnestness of the feeling of simultaneity with disaster, manual labor, and physical love, and of luxuriated futility permit poet-reader identification along the lines of what she declares in a self-explication of her earlier poem "The Swan": "Make sure there is nothing in the poem that would keep the reader from becoming the speaker of the poem." In this she mostly succeeds, even as most of us would never be *able* to write what she writes.

That Oliver has over the course of a thirty-year career consistently maintained close contact with what Emerson calls an "occult relation" between the human and the "vegetable" (which, for her sake we will broaden to include fauna) doesn't much need saying. But when invited by a new collection to do a kind of retrospective in the absence of a new *New and Selected*, one is fortunate to hear a richer totality emerging, particularly as her recent books have become increasingly retrospective and interwoven, or, we might say, introspective and retrowoven.

I'll choose as my framing line Rilke's most famous, which appears in

"Invitation" in *Red Bird* at the tail-end of the poem, as affirmation that one shouldn't ignore the noisy bustle of passerines in a hedge, a "rather ridiculous performance":

> It could mean something.
>
> It could mean everything.
>
> It could be what Rilke meant, when he wrote:
>
> *You must change your life.*

Let's pause to consider, then, an unconventional answer to that imperative: that a change in outlook and deliberate living might well correspond, as Helen Vendler strongly implies, to a change in poetic style. In this sense, and ironically, Oliver's lines above follow one of her beloved stanzaic structures: beveled quatrains with relatively short lines.

In this cluster of recent books she moves away from certain longstanding practices to embrace, firstly, prose poems. These do not much read like prosified versions of her lineated verse, often mounting a different take on her highly pedagogical nature-materialism, as in "The Word" in *What Do We Know* (2002), which imagines a half-Romantic, half-Zen scene of instruction in which members of an audience alternately listen intently to her speech about the soul or peel off by sevens to seek the experience she has been extolling. In some instances, like *Swan*'s "In Provincetown, and Ohio, and Alabama," one gets the sense that Oliver's plainspokenness might well short-circuit what Robert Bly calls the "half-hidden thoughts" of the prose poem. Two stanza-paragraphs respectively delineate the natural and manmade mortality of winter and the resuscitations of spring, as unspecified yellow flowers grow up around and through the carcass-skeleton of a "holy mule." The painful juxtaposition of memento mori and spring's irrepressible showing forth is more memorably and efficiently cast in the first lines of *The Waste Land* and in Roethke's dense, gnarled "Cuttings" and "Cuttings, Later."

Seemingly catching another trendy wave, Oliver tries her hand at a quartet of non-traditional "sonnets," three of which are comprised of twelve staggered lines that recall W. S. Merwin's steady minimalism in *The Vixen* and the instability of C. K. Williams's sprawling lines calculated to break at the margins to leave fragments dangling, as one can see in this middle "quatrain" from the first of them:

> Finally it opened its sheets of chitin and
>
> flew away.
>
> Linnaeus probably had given it a name, which I
>
> didn't know. All I could say was: Look
>
> what's come from its home of dirt and dust
>
> and duff, its

cinch of instinct. What does music, I wondered,

mean to it?

This is my favorite passage in the book by far, not merely because she shows here a willingness to break from her bare plainspokenness to weave in such striking repetitions of the short-*i*, but also because it feels genuine in its delight at the material of nature while offering a less irritating challenge to naming and knowing names—she has elsewhere warned of the dangers of the fanaticism of knowledge. More notable, ultimately, than the prose poems and late interest in sonnet-as-little-song is the increasing adoption of the resolute wisdom and the cadences of recent translations of Li Po, Hafiz, and Rumi, as in the uncompromisingly confident: "let me never be afraid to use the word *beautiful*."

In these late poems there is also an increasing tension between the deliberate change one might possibly seek and the inescapable changes wrought by time, particularly in relationship to the body. Oliver is capable of precious self-deprecation about the increasing limitations of the body ("Onward, old legs!"), delighted surprise at the persistence of the spirit (suddenly, after thirty years, she begins whistling again), and clear-eyed confrontation with death. At times she seems to abide by her declaration in *What Do We Know* that "Willingness is next to godliness," that for the time being she is content to dart and play, "agile and insistent" like a sparrow toying with a drifting feather, and will eventually be equally content to be more like the latter, "and just float away." But for the time being, she must be squarely corporeal, and some of the most successful moments in this book come when Oliver startlingly takes her being "full of beans" her whole life and lets her whimsy metamorphose into something veritably serious. "We eat the blessed earth," she admits in "Beans Green and Yellow," but truly shocks as she describes receiving the gift of a whitebark pinecone picked from the scat of a grizzly, which in a compulsive, uncanny, abject act she swallows herself, imagining its track through the "rough / and holy body" not just of the grizzly but also her own. The sheer unthinkability of such an act outstrips a lot of younger poets' sensationalistic bizarrism, and challenges us: ask not what is the most ridiculous thing you would do for attention, but to what lengths will your convictions and deepest subconscious urges drive you? Would you admit, "Okay... so I rescued a seagull with a broken wing"? Oliver does. Would you brood on killing two mosquitoes (in exasperation) and one spider (inadvertently)? In this sense, Oliver evades the charge of being mere nature poet, and her half-self-accusation of "negligence of mind" is not merely about reconnecting with nature but undercutting our nice bourgeois self-satisfactions.

In these and other moments one is called to Emerson again, though not merely as correlative but as contrast. If, as he says, "There is no object so foul that intense light will not make it beautiful" and "Every natural fact is trivial until it becomes symbolical or moral," it is sometimes frustrating that Oliver concentrates on conventional poetic flora and fauna, despite her too-often wan attempts at spinning them in new ways. The same is unfortunately true of her poems about her short-lived dog Percy, which appear in *Thirst* (2006), *Red Bird*, and *Swan*. Palpable pathos emerges in only three of the series—one in which one of Percy's kidneys is found to be nonfunctional and she broods on having named him after a poet who died young, rather than naming him for Wordsworth, who "almost never died"; the second in which Percy finds the company of other dogs at the shore whereas Oliver abjures the company of the other dogs' owners (or neglects to tell us about it); and the third in which Percy, having died, surges forth in her memory as she tries to explain the human habit of thinking: "His eyes questioned such an activity." We are, for better and for worse, beset by thinking, in all its recursiveness. How better, then, to cap *Swan* than with the title poem, at once a dark rewrite of Yeats's "A rush, a sudden wheel" in an early version of "Leda and the Swan," and again Rilke, not in the imperative but in the interrogative, to which there can really only ever be the honest, depressing answer: "And have you changed your life?"

Mary Biddinger, *Saint Monica*. Copper Canyon Press 2011. 42 pp, $22. Reviewed by Melissa Studdard

In what initially seems to be an arbitrary decision, Mary Biddinger's most recent poetry collection, Saint Monica, is dedicated to all girls whose names start with the letter "M." However, the significance of the dedication quickly becomes clear on two important counts: 1) as a way of establishing the adolescent protagonist, Monica, as a Catholic school Everygirl, and 2) as an echo of the day Monica (along with all other girls having names beginning with "M") was chosen to march in her school's May Crowning procession. Because Monica was both on display and lumped in with all the other schoolgirl "Ms" that day, the procession becomes a perfect symbol of the combined sense of anonymity and conspicuousness most adolescents feel. This motif runs through the rest of the collection, as Monica navigates bravely through the desires and embarrassments of pubescent social and personal life, vividly transporting us back to our own awkward years on a journey that we are, surprisingly, willing to take. It's a testimony to Biddinger's careful poetic crafting and deep understanding of the human psyche that what could start, for many, as an unwelcome trip, becomes a beautiful unfolding of empathy and compassion.

It's also no surprise that Monica's namesake is not a saint of purity and ease, but, rather, Saint Monica, the long-suffering wife of the violent tempered Patricus, and mother of the brilliant, unruly, Saint Augustine. In fact, Saint Monica has traditionally served as the patron of a motley crew of abuse victims, alcoholics, difficult marriages, disappointing children, homemakers, housewives, married women, mothers, victims of adultery, victims of verbal abuse, widows, and wives. Thanks to Biddinger, she also now serves as the symbol of a Midwestern schoolgirl's ability to bear down and mature through the strange and conflicting messages delivered through a haze of hormones, gossip, school lessons, parental advice, and fledgling intuition.

The loosely narrative poems and prose poems are conveyed from a third person limited point of view, which is especially poignant in the context of Monica's life, as it recreates the paradoxically angst-ridden but innocent tone of youth. We feel simultaneous distance and intimacy, timidity and boldness, comprehension and confusion as we remember what it means to live within the uncertainty of an adolescent mind. We are, with Monica, spun into a world of crushes, insecurities, hopes, disappointments, and questions. Masterfully, Biddinger grounds this swell of thought and emotion with visceral, tangible, concrete images and details. Monica's is a world of bubble gum, lip gloss, plaid skirts, Skoal, cordovan Hush Puppies, Kool Aid, tropical wine coolers, mini cupcakes, and training bras. Like pillows from home on a road trip, material items provide comfort and familiarity to the reader, and objects are called not just by name, but by brand name.

Emphasizing the youthful need for regularity and normalcy, the language of Saint Monica rarely becomes figurative, leaving poetic development to the larger aspects of structure—jagged, enjambed lines, symmetrical stanzas, and angular, muscular prose. As well, the overall style is cohesive, clean, controlled, and set in comforting contrast to the unpredictable world of our contemporary Saint Monica. It is a style that cradles the narrative, much in the way the Catholic school system cradles the children, by begging to redeem the lack of consistency and reliability of the adolescent experience with rules, structure, and conformity. The following excerpt from the previously mentioned May Crowning procession prose poem, "Saint Monica Stays the Course," is a perfect example of this:

> One year at Saint Joseph, the girls who had first names beginning with M were invited to walk in the May Crowning Procession. The Blessed Virgin stood at the side of the altar waiting to be topped with vines and lilies of the valley. Sister Cathleen instructed the girls in the correct way to proceed. Everyone had to wear white, of course, and no eyelet lace unless it was lined underneath. No ribbons in colors other than blue, for the Virgin. Monica's mother had stayed up all night stitching an empire-waist smock with puff sleeves that were perky but bulbous. Sister Cathleen measured hems with a metal ruler beforehand. Sister Cathleen said: whatever happens, do not stop marching. Do not look into the pews to smirk at your best friend or your brother. Keep your eyes on the Virgin. Clasp your bunch of daffodils, but don't clasp it too hard or the heads will shoot off and distract the other girls. Monica practiced this, the hard enough but not too hard, on a limp feather duster at home. Sister Cathleen instructed: do not stop this procession, whatever happens. If Molly Grace faints on the steps and suffers a concussion on impact, breaking her glasses, keep marching. If Maeve erupts in her first period, like a weather balloon tossed on a bed of thumbtacks, keep marching. If Meaghan and Melanie collide in front of the altar, white Mary Janes interlocking, proceed as planned. Magdalena may vomit up her cornflakes once she is seated in the pews. She has done this before. Keep your eyes to yourself. [...]

Here we see the control of diction that so perfectly mirrors the Catholic school environment and teachings, and we learn that the procession is a training ground for bearing out the difficulties these kids' futures are sure to bring. It's as though Saint Monica herself were standing before these girls teaching them how to stay the course of their lives, teaching them that through even the worst of disasters, the solution is simple: "Proceed as planned." Problems will arise aplenty, but a "good" girl keeps moving forward as if everything were in order.

Even the poem titles are symmetrical and controlled, with every single title in the collection starting with the words, "Saint Monica." Yet within that structure, we see, unfolding, poem by poem, the raw and feverish tale of Monica's coming of age, and with it a very subtle reminder of the irony of trying to impose order on anything. Monica's is that most epic and ordinary of tales, and like a series of images on a reel, the poems show us fragments of her life, woven together in a story that is both arbitrary and of universal, archetypal importance, a poetic reminder of who we are and who we were, and how to stay our course.

Jean Valentime, *Break the Glass*. Copper Canyon Press 2010. 81 pp. $22. Reviewed by Amanda Auchter

Jean Valentine's eleventh collection, *Break the Glass,* seeks to uncover the human—both literally (as in the "Lucy" poems) and figuratively. These poems, which appear as lyrical fragments of sorts, build to a discovery of what holds us together and what keeps us apart. An ancient skeleton which stands "about like a wildflower" is still as much a human as the speaker in "Even all night long" who, alone in the bed, reaches "across the sheet // anyone's hand / my face anyone's face." Valentine renders the human of *Break the Glass* as almost mythical in that it transcends time and location and is the "you" as seen in "In prison," "who the earth was for."

In the poem "Earth and the Librarian," the Earth becomes synonymous with Holy Communion:

> At the library
>
> she passed a tray with little
>
> books of baked earth on it—
>
>
> —Take one,
>
> and eat it;
>
> It is sweet,
>
> and it is given for you.

In return, the earth wonders "who lives in me?" The "take" and "eat" is reminiscent of the Catholic Rite of Communion in which the congregation is offered to "take this and eat" the body of Christ that "has been given up for you." In this, Valentine draws a stark parallel between the Earth and Christ. The Earth is "given for" the human that now offers its baked depiction on a tray. The Earth is an offering, it is "sweet," but still, Valentine's poem questions, who "lives in" or provides for the Earth? The Earth, here, is not entirely selfless and desires—as so many of the voices in these poems desire—to be connected to something or someone else, to not just be a thing "offered" or remembered.

The idea of wanting to be tied to something or someone else is a theme that Valentine's poems return to again and again in *Break the Glass*. Valentine skillfully uses the image of sewing and thread throughout the work to bind these fractured stories and voices together, even where they are separated by space and time. "I sit at a table / writing a letter / with a needle and thread," Valentine writes in the poem "If a Person Visits Someone in a Dream, in Some Cultures the Dreamer Thanks Them," dedicated to the poet Reginald Shepherd.

The book's title is integral to the poem, "If a Person Visits Someone in a Dream, in Some Cultures the Dreamer Thanks Them." The speaker of this poem writes to the deceased "with a needle and thread" and "on a bedspread" that he may "*breathe deeply and easily*." This wish is reminiscent of Valentine's tender concern for the other humans in the book: the women prisoners "in prison / without being accused// or reach your family / or have a family" ("In prison), the Earth, the coyotes whose howling is, to the speaker, "[s]exual love / coyotes crying / breathing close" ("Coyotes). Valentine's poems are filled with this desire for closeness in all its forms. Take, for example, the following from "If a Person Visits Someone in a Dream, in Some Cultures the Dreamer Thanks Them":

> Can you breathe all right?
>
> Break the glass   shout
>
> break the glass   force the room
>
> break the thread   Open
>
> the music behind the glass.

This is perhaps the most moving section in the entirety of the poem, if not the collection. "I call it dream," Valentine continues in the poem. Throughout *Break the Glass,* Valentine speaks as though from a dream or a vision in which this world is separated from another—the dead, the spiritual, memory—only by a thin thread or glass.

Valentine returns to the idea of separation by glass in the "Lucy" poems. These poems function as the centerpiece of *Break the Glass* and began as a thematic series in the chapbook, *Lucy,* published by Sarabande Books' Quarternote Chapbook Series. In this series, in which each poem-fragment is untitled, Valentine writes: "But you are my skeleton mother, / I bring you / coffee in your cemetery bed."

Lucy, in these poems, is the thread that binds Valentine's modern voice to the mystery of the past. The "skeleton mother" is revered and brought coffee even though she is without hands, "only / breath marks // breath marks / only." Lucy is representative of memory, of longing for understanding and connection. "What do you do now Lucy // for love?" ask Valentine, "[y]our eyeholes." Lucy, like the poems in Valentine's collection are filled with seeing, with love, with "breath marks" that give testimony to a life lived.

Just as glass when broken fragments, so do the stories in Valentine's intelligent, lyrically-wrought eleventh collection. The fragmentation in *Break the Glass* works well with the idea of how fractured humans are and in Valentine's world, humans are fractured in numerous ways: relics of bones of the three-million-year-old hominid Lucy, ghosts, prisoners without families, even the way the speaker in "Coyote" hears these animals howling in "the drought-country dark." In the poem 'Time is matter here," Valentine writes:

And you are matter—

your eyes, your long legs,

slow breath sometimes catching

in your sleep, your head

resting against the bus window

Here, Valentine speaks to the very essence that holds all humans together: the essential matter, the eyes, the legs, the breath, of each being that inhabits the world. The image of the head "resting against the bus window" is simple in its quiet portrayal: the "you" of the poem could be anyone (and it is, as Valentine quietly postulates, everyone).

"You can't get beauty," Valentine writes in "Then Abraham," "([s]till / in its longing it flies from you." Valentine's *Break the Glass* is filled with beauty in unexpected, memorable places. The poems create beauty where none is imagined: a matchbook in "Traveler," a letter written with needle in thread, a skeleton of a three million year-old woman. *Break the Glass* is the answer to a world so filled with disconnection and forgetting. These poems remember each part of the world and the world itself and create life from them with Valentine's gorgeous lines. "Do we get another life" writes Valentine in "Diana," "*Oh yes. / Maybe not in this place. Maybe in a different form.*"

Gerry LaFemina

A Book of Revelations: Secrets, Revelation and Character in the Lyric Poem

In fiction, of course, it is usual to discuss the nature of character; it has been said that in the short story character is revealed and in the novel character is explored–and by "character," of course, we are referring to one or more participants of action in the narrative. The epiphany of the short story is a moment when the protagonist should have (and, surely, the reader has) some new insight. The novel, on the other hand, seems to demand that the protagonist engage his/her behaviors and motivations and the world, and, in so doing, the essence of the character is explored. This is, of course, not a blanket statement; it is a matter of scope. The longer the narrative, the greater the ability to delve into the possibilities and nuances of a character's character.

And character is destiny, as Heraclitus reminds us.

Fiction is the obvious place to talk about character in this way, so it may seem strange that I want to spend time now discussing character and poetry. Many poems don't have characters, per se, at least not in the way we think of them in terms of fiction. And even those that do, most lyric poems don't have the arc of a storyline, and therefore the role of the "characters" seems, at least at first glance, of secondary import; however, I want to argue that character is a crucial aspect of poetry, and that in poetry character is transcended. One definition of the lyric experience–that held moment, which is brought to life in the lyric poem–is pure revelation, pure epiphany. It is an epiphanic moment removed from most of its narrative bindings. Take, for instance, this short poem by Larry Levis that I often discuss in class:

Wound

I've loved you

like a man loves an old wound

picked up in a razor fight

on a street nobody remembers.

Look at him:

even in the dark he touches it gently.

In this poem there are two characters–the lyric I and an unnamed you. Narrative in this poem is implicit. We know the relationship is over, and the lyric moment– the epiphany, as it were–is in the last line: the tenderness of the metaphoric touch lets us know the speaker still remains in love with the you.

So we have a protagonist (the lyric I) and an antagonist (the you): the force of change in the poem. The rest is secret. The form of the poem hints at some things: the stanzas reaffirm the separation between the couple, the enjambment throughout the first stanza and across the stanza break implies the speaker reaching across a distance, and the three end-stopped lines of stanza two shows a dismissal of that reaching out. But the details, the depth of the relationship, the back story: all of that remains secret. This forces the reader to engage his/her imagination, experiences, in order to help make meaning in the poem. As Hemingway says about stories: "the omitted part would strengthen the story and make people *feel* something more than they understood" (emphasis mine). The goal of the lyric poem is to get us to feel as if we've come to some insight, to some understanding, to some revelation—in other words, the goal is to have something new for both the poet and the reader, as Frost might say, which makes this idea of secret more than just exposure or poetic exhibitionism. Thus it's the search for this secret through which the writer and reader share an experience. Jacques Maritain, in his collected Mellon Lectures on Fine Arts *Creative Intuition in Art and Poetry*, believes poetry is "that intercommunication between the inner being of things and the inner being of the human Self which is a kind of divination (as was realized in ancient times; the Latin *vates* was both poet and diviner)" (3). We read poetry, in part, to be a part of this divination, to eavesdrop on this intercommunication and thus have access to the inner or secret being of things and the Self.

It's the secret, then, that gives the poem some of its power for both writer and reader. Secrets are defining and secrets pique the curiosity of others. People will do amazing things to avoid having their secrets revealed and to reveal the secrets of others. Surely, secrets are an important aspect of character. Charles Baxter once told a class of my students that some what he likes to know about characters include ten things everyone knows about him/her, and the ten things no one knows. The secrets don't need to be big—most of ours are. Our guilty pleasures, our small foibles, our own complicities in the day-to-day are all secrets that we may not want revealed. And like freemasons or brotherhood magicians, we don't want our secrets out. Poems are a type of magic making, and there's a tension built in the fundamental antithesis between revelation and secretiveness where a poem's power may be located. The poems that interest me are poems that seem to be both revealing something and hiding something simultaneously. They provide insight into character, without providing too much. They both capture the attention of the reader by seeming to provide revelation while simultaneously obscuring what exactly has been revealed.

James Wright's "A Blessing" exemplifies this balance. It's a deceptively simple poem, deceptive because its ending allows us to experience the speaker's conditional joy at the epiphany (emphasized by the "if") even as so much is absent from the poem. For instance, how this new-found knowledge works, what has happened so that the speaker feels like he would "break/into blossom" is completely left out of the poem. The tension in the poem (and thus for the reader) is kept secret even as the character's tension is broken.

However, the poem can't be pure secret. Just as the magician needs the audience to look away at the right moment and therefore needs to engage the audience throughout, the poet needs to allow the reader access into the context of the lyric experience: only by knowing something is at stake in the poem can the reader believe the insight of the epiphany. Because poetry doesn't usually provide the back story and characterization of fiction, there is a bit of Whitman's "What I assume you shall assume" sensibility in the lyric poem, and the poet needs to provide the reader with clues enough to allow the reader to feel the lyric experience without exposing the secrets themselves.

Consider, for instance, the connect-the-dots puzzles that children do. By connecting the numbers, a picture is drawn; the good poem provides enough dots that keep us reading and help us fill in the blanks. Too few dots, the poem fails to engage; too many, the poem loses its tension. In "A Blessing" there is a lot hinted at, which helps the reader "understand" the power of the last line; a close reading shows how Wrights embeds the clues–formally, structurally, imagistically– within the poem. For instance, although we know none of the back story as to why they have stopped "here," the poem is structured with two Indian ponies that balance the two people in the poem. This balance (which is further emphasized structurally by the number of sentences that span two lines–the entire first half of the poem) allows us to see that it's not so much that the horses love each other but still experience loneliness, so much as it is a reflection of the speaker's emotional sensibility.

It's important to keep in mind that the speaker of Wright's poem is a *character*, and, even if he shares a multitude of traits with James Wright the man, the speaker is an alter-ego, a construct, created in part by the discovery of voice. Realize, we are surrounded by people with multiple identities they keep separate. I am always amazed, for instance, how my students see me off campus somewhere– perhaps at a bar–; they often ask "What are you doing here?" because they are not expecting to see "me" there because my identity as a college professor is a construct established for the audience of the classroom. Ditto, I speak differently with my friends than I do with my family. The speaker of the poem is another construct, developed, in part to explore the secrets that language and image and craft–those elements that combine to create that thing we call voice–hint at.

The role of voice in the lyric poem is less a reflection of personality than it is an aspect of character, that element of the poet/speaker that has something at stake. If there's a failure in some contemporary poetry, it's that many poets confuse personality and character. We have a glut of poetry that is glib and driven by a speaker/self with little at stake. Adrienne Rich notes that even when writing from personal experience "if the imagination is to transcend and transform experience it has to question, to challenge, to conceive of alternatives, be free to play around with the notion that day might be night, love might be hate; nothing can be too sacred for the imagination to turn into its opposite or to call experimentally by another name. For writing is renaming" (43). By making such changes, of course, one is choosing–either consciously or intuitively– one's revelations.

The mistake many readers make (and many novice writers make) is the assumption that the speaker in the poem is the poet, and that the narrative context of the poem is the factual truth. In part, I blame the Confessional poets for this. Not because they told factual truths in their poems but because their name made it sound like they were spilling their guts out.

Anne Sexton is one who was often criticized for being too revealing, that she holds nothing back and that the poetry suffers from it. No doubt, in her mid-career poems in particular, when the personality Anne Sexton was more important than the poet Anne Sexton, this is true. But what that criticism touches upon is this very nature of the secret–the reader doesn't want to know everything, but wants to feel privy to *something*. And this is the balancing act for a poet. Sexton says in one interview: "I write a very personal poem but I hope they become the central theme to someone else's private life." (50) The act of revelation and withholding is something, then, that is shared between poet and audience when it's done right. Perhaps this is why she says in another interview, when asked what advice she would give to a young poet: "Tell *almost* the whole story" (109) (emphasis mine).

Let's consider, though, this poem by Sexton:

Just Once

Just once I knew what life was for.

In Boston, quite suddenly, I understood;

walked there along the Charles River,

watched the lights copying themselves,

all neoned and strobe-hearted, opening

their mouths as wide as opera singers;

counted the stars, my little campaigners,

my scar daises, and knew that I walked my love

on the green side of it and cried

my heart to the eastbound cars and cried

my heart to the westbound cars and took

my truth across a small humped bridge

and hurried my truth, the charm of it, home

and hoarded these constants into morning

only to find them gone.

This poem begins with its desire to reveal a secret: the speaker knew what life was for–and we expect to have that shared with it. But like enlightenment, we learn by the poem's end, that once you know you're enlightened you already have lost it. So she keeps this secret even though the poem begins with a gesture toward revelation.

Still, we feel as if something has been revealed–the emotional truth of having that treasure, the authentic loss of having lost it, and the real greed of wanting to hoard the truth, the knowledge, the self: in other words, the poem is about how important secret is to character, and dare I say it to Character.

And really, that's what I have been hoping to say all along: that the best poems have to work with the secrets of Character and what's beyond it–whether it is the Character of the thing (as in "Ode to a Grecian Urn" with its wonderful secretive last line), or the Character of a landscape, or the Character of the speaker-poet. Levis says in an interview:

> [Character] is a vital mask over the consistency or persistency of neuroses or madness, of being floored by being. That's what character is, a vast defense mechanism. . . . And it is . . . heroic in a social circumstance. But if you've ever been confronted by someone who has no defenses–who is *beyond* character, who is certainly beyond caring about all that, who's totally human and who asks you something so honest, probably the most honest question in your life–that's something else. What I'm talking about is finding a way to combine the two things, to have character (you can't get *away* from your own, anyway) and to ask something with the unbelievable honesty of a man who is about to vanish from the world. (110)

If Character is a defense mechanism, perhaps the character we develop–that voice we take on in the lyric poem–is a way to transcend our Character, to be as honest as possible. But because we can't escape our own Character, the best poems–the most authentic poems–maintain their secrets while providing insight for the reader into character. Mark Strand puts it this way:

> Good poems . . . have a lyric identity that goes beyond whatever their subject happens to be. They have a voice and the formation of that voice, the gathering up of imagined sound into utterance may be the true occurrence for their existence. A poem may be the residue of an inner urgency, one through which the self wishes to register itself, write itself into being, and, finally, to charm another self, the reader, into belief. (43)

Lyric identity might be synonymous with character in this instance, different from self or personality.

Consider the sometimes charming voice of Tony Hoagland's poems–which seem in their conversational nature, in their wry, matter-of-fact narratives to be revealing only the snarky nature of the intellectual, artsy outsiders of Hoagland's world. Yet, in Hoagland's best poems there's a sense of self awareness about this pose, a knowing, ironic wink to the reader that suggests there is something under the surface in all this. Take, for instance, these lines from "Argentina":

Karth says February is always like eating a raw egg;

Peter says it's like wearing a bandage on your head;

Mary says it's like a pack of wild dogs who have gotten into medical waste, and smiles because she clearly is the winner.

And in Argentina, after the elections,

we hear the old president won't leave office–

literally, they say–they can't get him out of the office!

He's in there with his little private army, eating caviar,

squandering state money on call girls and porno movies–

and if you've done any therapy at all, I think you'll see the analogy.

How did I come to believe in a government called Tony Hoagland?

with an economy based on flattery and self-protection?

and a sewage system of selective forgetting?

and an extensive history of broken promises?

There's a cleverness in Hoagland's rhetoric, and his characters (Hoagland's poems are filled with characters), who sound simultaneously smart and sensitive, are equally as clever. But Hoagland hints that there's a shallowness under the surface (how Mary grins at being "the winner") that he won't explore because "if you've done any therapy" the reader will understand. So we experience secret and revelation. Hoagland's chatty rhetoric, his use of long lines at times, captures a kind of nervousness–or perhaps, more accurately, insecurity– that seems to embody Levis's notion of fusing character and brutal, can't-help-but-be-anything-but honesty. In other words, what Sexton calls "authenticity."

What could be more authentic–more human–than having a secret and wanting to share it and keep it both? John Berger notes that "Authenticity in literature does not come from a writer's personal honesty ... Authenticity comes from a single faithfulness: that to the ambiguity of experience" (Qtd in Dunn 146).

One place where that ambiguity manifests itself is in rhetoric–in how our speaker speaks. Stephen Dunn suggests that poets need to have "a greater awareness that first-person narrators are also characters and must be treated as such by their authors" (147). By thinking of the speaker as character, a poet can distance him/herself from the secrets, to find the secrets of the poem, and one way to do this is to consider the attitude of the speaker toward the subject matter and toward the self. Rhetoric, obviously, is an element of craft–one that often falls by the wayside or is lumped into the sense of a speaker's "voice" when discussing poems, but rhetoric is truly representative of the character of the speaker, his/her attitude toward subject matter, and how much insight he/she is willing to provide. Consider how Denise

Duhamel approaches subject matter via a kind of approach-and-avoidance strategy; I'm thinking of her poem "Cockroaches," which begins with a statement of fact—that her father-in-law refers to "American kids" who backpack across Europe as "cockroaches" and how she won't share with him the details of her summer as a cockroach (though she does share them with the reader). She claims:

> I can't tell him these things because he is old
>
> and elegant and embarrasses easily, knows about tax
>
>
> shelters and deutsche marks and yen. Besides, he shares
>
> what he has with me. O.K. It's true—technically
>
> cockroaches are more active in summer months, but some believe
>
> they can also cure skin ulcers when ground and mixed with sugar.

The line breaks tell us some things—"It's true—technically" is meant to be read not only as part of its sentence, but also as part of what comes beforehand. There's more to what the speaker feels—about the father-in-law, but it's withheld. It's secret. And instead, the poem will now circumambulate the secrets, giving us insight into the speaker's sense of insecurity around the father-in-law.

Duhamel has already established a notion that there is a disconnect here, and it's suggested it has to do with class "embarrassment": the poem moves from the cockroaches, to the speaker's observations of how roaches died in her apartment ("on their backs") to some of the ways to kill them. Then the poem moves again:

> Roaches—that's what we called the boys next door
>
> whose last name was Rochelle, whose father was a circus clown
>
> with a bad temper when his make-up was off, whose above-the-
>   ground
>
> pool perched in their driveway—the dirty water, pea soup
>
> thickened with ham hock. "*La cucaracha, la cucaracha,*"
>
> my sister and I sang as the younger brother peed
>
> into their cat's litter box....

The circus clown is most telling—as circus clowns openly live the lives of two identities: the public persona of the clown, and the private self that only his children and the neighbors see. The speaker then muses that her father-in-law might have seen her then the way she looked at the Rochelle boys, until admitting "We were cockroaches, happy as all the rest/ scurrying fast across this dirty tub we knew as America."

Despite the sincere tone of the poem, the speaker's willingness to not train the focus of her attention on any particular aspect of the topic suggests more avoidance–something hidden beneath the revelation. This is particularly easy to believe when one considers Duhamel's willingness to take on fairy tales, Barbie, Innuit folk stories, etc, as subject matter. One may note a desire that she has to both find the potential secrets in these artifacts for a contemporary American audience and to find some cultural secret through such lenses, but one may also think of it as a willingness to veil revelation of the self with the skein of such subject matter, much the way some readers look at Sexton's last few books. Alicia Ostriker notes about Sexton's poems (from *Transformations* in this case–her retelling of fairy tales): "What she does with this material is seize it, crack it open and *make* it personal. The result is at once . . . interpretation and a valid continuation of the folklore tradition– and a piece of poetic subversion whereby the 'healthy' meanings we expect to enjoy are held up to icy scrutiny" (65). In other words, writers working with such material attempt to find out the secret meaning that exists in the work for themselves as reader and present that via their own writing.

It should be noted, however, that what the secret is is often unknown to the self (you would know this "if you have done any therapy at all"): this is why writing to discover is so important. As Frost noted, "I write to find out what I didn't know I knew," and it's in those secrets where we find the most energy for our poems–that discovery of secret lives, whether real or imagined. There are, of course, other secrets within character: landscape poets may seek to discover the secrets of a geography's landscape (a secret closely related to the secrets of the speaker experiencing that landscape); ditto, the great object poems of the Deep Imagist movement attempted to find the secret character of familiar objects (just as the Imagist poets attempted similarly to make us reconsider the character of certain objects). "What matters to us," Maritain notes, "is the mutual entanglement of nature and man–let us say, the coming together of the World and the Self–in relation to artistic creation. Then we truly enter our subject matter. And then we have to do with Poetry" (9). The character of the speaker–that figure who is already in his/her make-up, who is a construct of the poet but also, by his/her very nature, an aspect of the poet–also begs to be examined, to have its secret character revealed.

The work of the poet, then, becomes one of negotiating all the potentialities of a poem– of content, form, rhetoric, image, narrative, the imagination, voice, syntax, etc– to lead himself and readers to some revelation, something that makes us feel an epiphany happened. Perhaps, ultimately, this is why I dislike thematic collections or distrust whenever a poet tells me they are working on a project, just as I dislike "concept" albums by bands. Usually the secret character of the theme binding such projects together is written out long before the collection is finished. Ditto, I dislike the poem of simple anecdote as it has no secret to hide. Its tension has been mitigated because it risks little, the revelations seem trite and expected. The poet's tone, the poet's willingness (or unwillingness) to engage what's concealed, leads to deeper water.

For me, poems fail when the writer refuses to engage the secret nature of things (and thus the speaker/self)–when images are imbued with little more than their ordinariness; they fail, too, when the fear of revelation leads the poet either to staying too close to the surface or else to obscuring the secret in such a way as to abstract the very transcendent process of revelation. Lastly, they fail when the secret is so fully revealed as to leave it powerless. We live in a culture of prying media, tell-all memoirs, paparazzi, and chronic Facebook updates—in which the private world is constantly on display. With this in mind, then, it is not, ultimately, in the thing revealed which gives a lyric poem its energy; rather, it's in the process, in the hint of revelation, in the craft that allows us to accept that magic happened—that the bird appeared from the bouquet of flowers, even when we know it only happened because, at the right time, the magician managed to get us to turn our heads.

Works Cited

Duhamel, Denise. "Cockroaches." *The Star-Spangled Banner.* Carbondale: SIU, 1999. 35-36.

Dunn, Stephen. "Journal Notes." *Walking Light.* Rochester: BOA Editions, 2001. 145-49.

Hoagland, Tony. "Argentina." *What Narcissism Means to Me.* Minneapolis: Graywolf, 2003.

Levis, Larry. "An Interview by David Wojahn." *The Gazer Within.* Ann Arbor: U Michigan, 2001. 88-111.

- - - . "Wound." *Wrecking Crew.* Pittsburgh: U Pitt, 1974.

Maritain, Jacques. *Creative Intuition in Art and Poetry.* Cleveland: Meridian Books, 1953.

Ostriker, Alicia. "That Story: the Changes in Anne Sexton." *Writing Like a Woman.* Ann Arbor: U Michigan, 1983.

Sexton, Anne. "Just Once." *Love Poems.* Boston: Houghton Mifflin, 1969.

- - -. No Evil Star. Steven E. Colburn, ed. Ann Arbor: U Michigan, 1985.

Strand, Mark. *The Weather of Words.* New York: Knopf, 2000.

Wright, James. "A Blessing." *The Branch Will Not Break.* Middletown: Wesleyan U, 1963. 57.

In the summer of 1986, I met the sheep who would change everything. I had been investigating Lancaster Stockyards, a sprawling Pennsylvania auction facility where hordes of frightened, exhausted animals were sold for fattening or slaughter. Many never made it to the auction floor. Those who died from the hardships of their lives on the farm, or from the harrowing journey to the yards, were dumped in a heap, called simply "the dead pile," to await the renderer. One sweltering day in August, as my partner and I approached that dumping ground, we saw a young sheep. Lying among carcasses that seethed with maggots, she appeared dead. But sensing someone nearby, she suddenly mustered the strength to lift her head. We knew immediately that we had to help her. In that moment, I was transformed from a witness into a rescuer.

Though we had little hope that the sheep would survive, we lifted her carefully into our van and left the stockyard looking for a veterinarian who could at least provide humane euthanasia. We finally found a veterinarian to examine our rescue. As he gently handled her, she began to perk up, and within twenty minutes she was standing, eating and drinking, and had come fully to life before our eyes. Hilda, as we later named her, was not suffering from any injuries or diseases. She had simply collapsed from the brutal conditions of her transport to the stockyard. She had been abandoned to die a slow death, though she needed only a little care and nourishment to revive. There were others like her, others we could save. And we would fight for the multitudes beyond the reach of direct rescue, aiming to end to the cruelty they endure in factory farms, stockyards and slaughterhouses. As Hilda found her legs, so did Farm Sanctuary.

While our first rescued animal regained her strength, we launched an investigation of Lancaster Stockyards. In 1993 our efforts led to the first ever conviction of a U.S. stockyard for mistreating a downed animal. This groundbreaking victory of our *No Downers* campaign was followed by others, including passage of a law in California, since emulated by other states, that prevents dragging, pushing, holding, or selling downed animals at stockyards and slaughterhouses. In 2009 the USDA finally locked in a nationwide rule to prohibit the slaughter of downed cattle. While lauding this step, we continue to fight for the downed pigs, goats, and sheep who still suffer horrific cruelty when they become downed at facilities throughout the country.

Meanwhile, other advocacy projects have also gained ground for farm animals. Through our *Anti-Confinement Campaign*, we have worked extensively on initiatives banning the industry's three most torturous confinement systems: battery cages for egg-laying hens, gestation crates for sows, and veal crates. These inhumane devices confine animals so tightly that they cannot walk, turn around, or stretch their limbs. In 2002, Farm Sanctuary was a key sponsor of Florida's gestation crate ban, the first U.S. ballot initiative to outlaw a cruel factory farming practice. In 2006, another Farm Sanctuary-backed ballot initiative succeeded when Arizona voters passed a ban on gestation and veal crates. Two years later, our efforts resulted in the most sweeping ballot-box victory when Californians voted overwhelmingly to ban gestation crates, veal crates, and battery cages in their state, impacting the lives of nearly 20 million animals. These victories engendered a trend: Legislation banning one or more confinement system has now been passed in Oregon, Colorado, Maine, and Michigan as well. In the summer of 2011, with Farm Sanctuary, the Humane Society of the U.S., and other groups challenging the egg industry in Oregon and Washington, the United Egg Producers agreed to support federal legislation to improve the welfare of all U.S. laying hens and eventually outlaw barren battery cages entirely. Industry's endorsement of this legislation – which will be the first federal law relating to the welfare of chickens used for food, the first federal law addressing the treatment of animals on factory farms, and the first farmed animal protection legislation in more than 30 years – illustrates the progress we have made and that agribusiness cruelties are indefensible and outside the bounds of acceptable conduct.

Our influence and impact have grown significantly over the past 25 years. Farm Sanctuary has come to be recognized as an authority on farm animal issues. When the first case of mad cow disease was discovered in the U.S., in 2003, Farm Sanctuary was sought out for comments by *New York Times, Los Angeles Times, Associated Press, Reuters, Taipei Times, CNN.com*, and others. The following year, Farm Sanctuary discussed animal rights at the U.S. Department of Agriculture (USDA), becoming the first animal protection organization to be invited to speak publicly on that topic before the agency.

Our voices have also grown in number. Crucial to the victories we have achieved for farm animals have been the many volunteers and supporters throughout the country who leant their time, labor, and passion to the fight. Galvanizing and equipping a growing body of advocates, particularly through our *Advocacy Campaign Team (ACT)*, is among our most important and rewarding work.

Hilda, who grew into a beautiful, healthy sheep, lived with

us for 11 years, first in the yard of a row house in Wilmington, Del., and eventually on the rolling, green pastures of the shelter we established outside Watkins Glen, N.Y. Others quickly joined her. Once we started our rescue efforts, there seemed to be no end to the abused, neglected, and abandoned animals in need of our help. As we grew, cattle, goats, sheep, pigs, chickens, turkeys, ducks, and geese found refuge with us. Herds and flocks established themselves among our barns. We gradually cultivated a nationwide community of adopters and fellow rescuers to enable even more rescues, creating the largest farm animal rescue and refuge network in North America. At the time of this writing, more than 8,000 animals have received sanctuary at our two internationally recognized shelters, and another 3,000 have reached permanent, loving homes through our *Farm Animal Adoption Network.*

After all these years and all these rescues, the transformations of the animals we save still amaze me. Some of the most poignant have been those of laying hens from battery cage facilities, where they spent every moment of their lives in dim barracks reeking of ammonia, crowded in tiny wire cages, unable even to stretch their wings. Released into a yard at our shelter for the first time, a battery-cage hen takes her first steps tentatively, somewhat warily. She has never walked more than a step or two in her life, never felt earth beneath her feet, never seen sunshine. And yet she is soon running, pecking in the dirt for insects, and fanning her wings wide to sunbathe. Intrinsic desires, relentlessly frustrated all her life, are suddenly realized. She remembers, joyfully, how to be a chicken.

Animals come to us ravaged by neglect and mistreatment: diseased, injured, and terrified. Those who sought to exploit these creatures have driven them from their right selves, but they can be brought back, and they can thrive. We've seen neglected goats, at first painfully timid of humans, become confident and curious. We've seen tiny, sickly piglets, at one time barely clinging to life, grow into healthy pigs whose robust cheerfulness lifts our own spirits. We have seen so many animals emerge from pain and hardship through the deep friendships they are able, when treated kindly, to form with each other and with their caregivers. And since our very first days, we've invited those around us to see what we see, because often the most profound change begins simply with one person and one animal, meeting one another.

Every year, thousands visit our shelters to volunteer, take tours, or stay overnight. For many, these experiences offer a first chance to come face to face with farm animals, and these encounters can be transformative. Visitors discover that some chickens are shy but others spunky, that giant steers can be gentle, and that geese can have best friends. Guests see the lingering scars of abuse and the tenacious spirit of survival. They see that each animal is unique, with as much personality and with as great a need and worthiness for kindness as a companion dog or cat. Some people come to us as omnivores, and tell us that, after meeting and learning about farm animals, they can never eat them again. Some who come to us already vegetarian or vegan tell us that they want to do more.

A critical function of our education program has been to catalyze such revelations, which can change the manner in which individuals live and which, in aggregate, can alter the tenor of our culture. In addition to our visitor program and the conferences and celebrations that draw people to our shelters, we have developed a number of educational initiatives to promote understanding of farm animals and awareness of their condition. Our celebrity collaborations draw public attention, and through our media outreach, we reach millions of people around the world. Events such as our annual *Adopt-A-Turkey Project* and *Walk for Farm Animals*, which both began quite humbly during our first year of operation, now galvanize thousands of participants across the country – raising vital funds, educating masses of people, and fostering a nationwide community of advocates united by concern for their fellow creatures. Though the members of this community may be separated by thousands of miles, the animals connect us all.

The factory farming industry attempts to reduce its victims, to change them from sentient beings into inanimate commodities. It does not succeed. Even in debasement, the internal lives of these animals persist. When animals have been rescued, healed, and given the safety and care they deserve, their internal lives flourish, manifesting in displays of affection, joy, and dignity. They are themselves. And this is a restoration of agency, for simply through being themselves, these creatures, more than mere victims or beneficiaries, have the power to stir a feeling of kinship in the human heart. They have the power to change minds, and habits, and lives. As the animals are transformed, so are we.

– Gene Baur, President & Co-Founder,

Farm Sanctuary

Since 1986 Farm Sanctuary, the nation's leading farm animal protection organization, has worked to end cruelty to farm animals and promote compassionate living. Farm Sanctuary rescues animals from abject cruelty, exposes the callousness and disregard for life that drive the "food animal" industry, and advocates for legal protections for farm animals. Help us protect the most vulnerable among us, and raise your voice in compassion for farm animals everywhere. To learn more about our shelters, campaigns and educational programs visit www.farmsanctuary.org.

25th Anniversary

farmsanctuary

rescue • education • advocacy

National Office · P.O. Box 150 · Watkins Glen, NY 14891 · 607-583-2225

www.farmsanctuary.org

Mary Biddinger is the author of *Prairie Fever* (Steel Toe Books, 2007) and Saint Monica (Black Lawrence Press, 2011). Her poetry has appeared in *32 Poems, Copper Nickel, diode, Gulf Coast, The Laurel Review, The National Poetry Review, North American Review, Passages North, Third Coast*, and many other journals. She is the editor of the Akron Series in Poetry and co-editor-in-chief of *Barn Owl Review.*

Julie Danho is an editor working in Providence, Rhode Island. Her poems have appeared in *Barrow Street, Southern Poetry Review, Cream City Review,* and *West Branch*, among others. She received an M.F.A. from Ohio State University and was recently awarded a Fellowship Merit Award in Poetry from the Rhode Island State Council on the Arts.

Edison Dupree's collection *Prosthesis* was published in the Bluestem Award series. Recent work appears in Salamander, Southern Poetry Review, and the *William and Mary Review*. He lives in Cambridge, Mass., and works as a library assistant at Harvard University

James Grinwis is the author of *The City from Nome* (The National Poetry Review Press, March 2011) and *Exhibit of Forking Paths* (Coffee House Press, November 2011), winner of the National Poetry Series. His work has appeared in *American Poetry Review, Black Warrior Review, Columbia, Third Coast*, etc.

Heather Kirn's poems have appeared in *Alaska Quarterly Review, Beloit Poetry Journal, Cincinnati Review*, and elsewhere. A Rona Jaffe-Bread Loaf Scholar in nonfiction, she has had essays noted in The Best American Essays Series and published in such places as *The San Francisco Chronicle, Fourth Genre, The Southern Review* and *Prairie Schooner*. She is a Visiting Assistant Professor of English at Miami University in Hamilton, Ohio.

Tracey Knapp lives in San Francisco, where she works in consulting and graphic design. Her poems have appeared or are forthcoming in *The New Ohio Review, Best New Poets 2010, Best New Poets 2008, Connotation Press, The Minnesota Review*, and elsewhere.

Gregory Lawless is a graduate of the Iowa Writers' Workshop and the author of *I Thought I Was New Here* (BlazeVOX). His poems, reviews and interviews have appeared in or are forthcoming from *2River View, Artifice, Best of the Net 2007, Cider Press Review, The Cortland Review, Drunken Boat, H_NGM_N, The Hollins Critic, InDigest, La Petite Zine, Sonora Review, Tarpaulin Sky, Thermos, Third Coast, Zoland Poetry* and others.

John Mann's poems have appeared in *Fence, Massachusetts Review, Northwest Review, Poetry International, Many Mountains Moving, Vallum, Eleventh Muse, The Literary Review, Confrontation, American Letters & Commentary, Birmingham Poetry Review, Burnside Review, Alaska Quarterly Review, Mid-American Review, The Fiddlehead, The Comstock Review, Main Street Rag, Tampa Review*, and *Crazyhorse*. Finishing Line Press published *Wyoming*, a chapbook of poems, in 2008.

April Manteris has an MFA from Florida State University, where she also received the Ann Durham Creative Writing Thesis Award. She is currently a PhD candidate and instructor at Florida State University.

Susan Rothbard's work has appeared in *Poet Lore, The Literary Review, Comstock Review, Pif Magazine, Dogwood, Paterson Literary Review* and other journals and has been featured on *Verse Daily*. She earned her MFA degree at Fairleigh Dickinson University.

Larry Sawyer curates the Myopic Poetry Series in Wicker Park, Chicago and edits milkmag.org. His poems have appeared in *Action Yes, Chicago Tribune, Court Green, Exquisite Corpse, MiPOesias, Shampoo, Skanky Possum, Van Gogh's Ear, Vanitas, Verse Daily,* and *VLAK*. His first full length collection is *Unable to Fully California* (Otoliths).

THE AMERICAN POETRY JOURNAL

APJ

ISSUE NUMBER ELEVEN

Sr. Editor:
J.P. Dancing Bear

Reviews Editor:
James Cihlar

Editor:
Dorine Jennette

Advisory Board:
Jennifer Michael Hecht
Bob Hicok
Jane Hirshfield
C. J. Sage
Diane Thiel

Subscriptions:
Individuals: $15.00 per year
Institutions: $20.00 per year
(Please add $6.00 postage per year for subscriptions outside the United States.)

Web site: www.americanpoetryjournal.com

The APJ reads magazine submissions online only.
Please see website for the latest guidelines.

Address submissions, queries, orders, and all other correspondence to:

J.P. Dancing Bear, Editor
The American Poetry Journal
Post Office Box 2080
Aptos, California 95001-2080

The American Poetry Journal Copyright 2011 All Rights
Reserved
ISSN 1547-6650
ISBN 978-1-935716-11-2

Cover art: "Testing" courtesy of Craig Kosak
www.craigkosak.com

The American Poetry Journal is a production of Dream Horse Press LLC

Reviews

TABLE OF CONTENTS

POETRY

www.ingramcontent.com/pod-product-compliance
Lightning Source LLC
Chambersburg PA
CBHW020921090426
42736CB00008B/743

* 9 7 8 1 9 3 5 7 1 6 1 1 2 *